Acknowledgements

I extend my heartfelt appreciation to you, the reader, for embarking on this journey with us. It's my sincere hope that Bella's story resonates with you as much as it has with me, and that it inspires you to 'buzz' in your own unique way.

As we turn the pages of this book, let's together turn the pages of our lives towards recognition, respect, and a thriving hive-like community, irrespective of where we are. The hive is, after all, not just a place but a feeling - one of belonging, appreciation, and shared growth.

table of Contents:

Every Buzz Counts 1
Nectar Now, Honey Later..3
A Constant Buzz Keeps The Hive Humming................6
Specific Buzz, Sweeter Honey..9
Buzz Out Loud, Inspire The Crowd................................12
Every Bee Deserves Their Buzz......................................15
Values In Our Buzz. Unity In Our Hive..........................17
Change The Buzz, Change The Hive..............................19
The Queens' Address..22
The Path Of The Hive..24
The Hive Rules..26

Chapter 1: Every Buzz Counts

As the first rays of dawn painted the sky, Bella found herself next to Willow on a petal-laden branch. The hum of the awakening hive served as a distant backdrop to their conversation.

"Bella, you seem quieter than usual. Is something bothering you?" Willow asked, her antennae twitching with concern.

Bella took a moment before responding, her wings softly fluttering. "Willow, do you ever feel... invisible? Like all our hard work is unnoticed?" Her voice was but a soft buzz, filled with a sadness that Willow rarely heard.

Willow gave a slow nod, pausing to clean her wings, a habit she picked up when deep in thought. "Sometimes, Bella. I think many of us do."

"It's just...I believe every buzz we make, every flower we visit...it counts. But it feels like no one else sees it that way." Bella looked at Willow, her compound eyes reflecting an earnest longing for change.

Willow touched her antennae to Bella's in a comforting gesture. "That's a powerful thought, Bella. Maybe it's not just about feeling seen, but about changing how we see each other. Recognition in the hive... everyone should give and receive it. **Every Buzz Counts**"

In that quiet conversation, a seed was planted. It was the beginning of Bella's journey, a journey that would transform the hive. Their conversation was more than just shared feelings; it was the spark of an idea that would light the path for change. Bella, though discontent, was on the brink of something profound.

Chapter 2: Nectar Now, Honey Later

In the heat of the summer, the hive was gripped by a troubling scarcity. Fields that were once abundant with nectar-bearing flowers now stood starkly barren. The buzz of worry was palpable within the hive's honeycomb corridors.

Amidst this, Bella, a worker bee driven by her innate sense of responsibility, flew tirelessly each day, her wings beating in sync with her heart, in search of new pollen-rich flowers. Her journey took her farther away from the hive, often venturing into territories unexplored by her fellow bees.

One sweltering afternoon, just when Bella's wings felt heavy and her hopes started to wane, she saw a sight that made her heart flutter with excitement - a vast, untouched garden glowing in the sunlight. It was an explosion of color, a symphony of fragrances. Sunflowers reached out to the sky in a joyful salute; tulips and daisies stood tall and proud, their petals boasting hues she had never seen before. It was an oasis in a desert, a beacon in the night.

Bella raced back to the hive, her heart pounding, eager to share her precious discovery. Bursting through the hive entrance, she navigated the intricate honeycomb pathways till she reached the royal chamber.

"Your Highness," Bella buzzed, her voice shaky with anticipation as she bowed to Queen Quentina. "I've found an untouched garden, a bounty of flowers waiting to be pollinated. It's rich in nectar and will solve our food problem."

Queen Quentina, majestic and commanding, listened attentively, her multifaceted eyes reflecting the urgency in Bella's voice. After a thoughtful pause, she said, "That is indeed promising news, Bella. However, we must discuss this in depth. We shall bring it up at our next hive meeting."

Days turned into a week, yet Bella's discovery remained unacknowledged. Her excitement gradually deflated like a balloon, replaced by a gnawing sense of disappointment. She felt overlooked and disconnected from the hive. She found herself whispering, "**Nectar now, Honey later**," realizing the importance of timely recognition.

Bella's monumental discovery had not just unearthed a new garden but also the shortcomings in the hive's recognition system. This realization stirred within her a resolve to bring about a transformation. Her journey was just beginning.

Chapter 3: A consistent buzz keeps the hive humming

In the lingering warmth of the early summer days, Bella found herself working shoulder to shoulder with Bruno, the respected bumblebee. They were stationed at the heart of the hive, within the golden-lit chambers where the transformation of gathered nectar into honey took place.

Their task was an intricate one, filled with precision and finesse. Bruno, with years of experience etched into his form, moved with a rhythm born of practiced repetition. Bella watched him work, marveling at the efficiency in his movements. Yet, she noticed a recurring pattern - Bruno's diligent efforts often went unseen, a silent echo of her own unacknowledged discovery.

It was on one such day, while they were tending to the sweet, sticky nectar, that Bella decided to voice her thoughts. "Bruno," she ventured, the hint of a question making her voice waver. "Do you ever feel... unheard?"

The question hung in the air, the steady hum of the hive wrapping around them. Bruno paused, his normally busy antennae stilling at Bella's words. "Heard, you say? Bella, in my time, the hive buzzes and we listen. It's not about one bee, it's about the hive," he mused, his voice a deep buzz that resonated in the chamber.

"But don't you think it should be about every bee too, Bruno?" Bella pressed, her compound eyes reflecting a passionate determination. "Every worker in the hive contributes, just like you. And every contribution is valuable, whether it's a single drop of nectar or a new flower patch."

There was a weighty pause. Bruno stopped his work, his gaze thoughtful as he considered Bella's words. "Yes, Bella," he said slowly. "A worker's efforts should be recognized. Not occasionally, but consistently. A steady rhythm of recognition could keep our hive strong."

This affirmation filled Bella with a new sense of purpose. "That's it, Bruno! '**A consistent buzz keeps the hive humming**.' Imagine if every small act, every effort was appreciated as it happened. It would create an environment where everyone feels seen and valued."

As the day turned into twilight, their conversation echoed within the golden chamber, intertwining with the humming buzz of the hive. It was not just a conversation between two bees; it was the beginning of a crucial change in their hive's recognition culture.

With every passing day, Bella was evolving from being just another worker bee to becoming an agent of transformation. This realization marked a turning point, a promise of a more inclusive and appreciative hive that honored the consistent efforts of its workers. Bella was ready to ensure that every buzz was heard.

Chapter 4: Specific buzz, sweeter honey

Summer was in full swing. The hive was a constant hum of activity, with worker bees buzzing to and fro. In the heart of this activity, Bella and Bruno were huddled together, their antennae twitching with concentration as they worked on Bella's latest innovation. Bella had devised a unique, efficient way to streamline honey production, an innovation that could revolutionize their hive.

Their fellow worker, Perry, a sprightly bee known for his jovial nature, was intrigued by their intense focus. "What's got you two buzzing so seriously?" he asked, fluttering over to join them.
"Bella's found a way to speed up honey production," Bruno explained, his voice filled with pride. "

"It's a new method that could save us time and energy.", Bellas face lit up with excitement as she explained.
Perry was visibly impressed. "That's incredible, Bella. We should share this with the hive at once!"

Energized by Perry's enthusiasm, Bella and Bruno presented their innovation at the next hive meeting. They explained the process in detail, from the precise manipulation of nectar to the delicate adjustments in temperature that would lead to faster, more efficient honey production.

There was a brief silence after Bella's presentation. Then, the generic buzz of acknowledgment filled the chamber, the equivalent of a collective nod. The reaction was lukewarm at best, the enthusiasm Bella had hoped for was missing.

"Good job, Bella," came the standard reply from the hive. But the response felt hollow to Bella. She had expected her innovation to spark a buzz, to make a difference. Instead, she was met with a blanket acknowledgment, void of any real appreciation or understanding of her hard work.

As the hive meeting disbanded, Bella, Bruno, and Perry reconvened. Bella felt a sinking feeling in her abdomen, the lukewarm response had dampened her spirits.

"Bruno, Perry, it's not about the praise," Bella voiced her feelings. "But wouldn't a specific acknowledgment make our efforts feel more meaningful? Just like how the specific buzz of a bee can identify it in the hive."

Bruno nodded, understanding Bella's sentiments. "You're right, Bella. The appreciation should reflect the effort. A specific buzz for a specific job."

Perry chimed in, "You've hit the nail on the head, Bella. **'Specific buzz, sweeter honey**.' That's exactly what we need. Your innovation deserved more than just a 'good job.' It's a game-changer."

The trio sat in thoughtful silence, the hum of the hive around them. Their conversation had sparked an important realization. A generic acknowledgment could never replace the value of specific recognition. Each worker's contribution was unique, and the recognition should be too.

That evening, under the soft, diffused light in the heart of the hive, Bella felt a renewed sense of purpose. She knew that her journey was far from over. With Bruno and Perry by her side, she felt ready to push for a culture where every bee's contribution would be specifically acknowledged, fostering a sweeter, more rewarding hive.

"The summer was growing warmer, but within the hive, the seeds of change had begun to take root. Bella's innovation may not have received the specific recognition it deserved, but it marked another significant step in her mission to transform the hive's culture. And with each step, she was growing more determined, more focused. Bella, Bruno, and Perry were on a mission, their resolve as steadfast as the summer sun.

Chapter 5: Buzz out loud, inspire the crowd

As the height of summer began to wane, the hive faced a new threat - a rogue wasp that had strayed too close to their home. Nina, a quick-thinking scout bee, was the first to spot the intruder. With unparalleled bravery, she took it upon herself to defend their home.

Nina darted forward, her wings beating a rhythm of courage. Her movements were swift and strategic, managing to distract the wasp long enough for the other bees to mobilize. The battle was short-lived but intense, and soon, the wasp retreated, buzzed away by Nina's relentless defense.

However, when Nina returned to the hive, her heroic feat went largely unnoticed. Bella, Bruno, and Perry, who had observed the confrontation, approached Nina, their antennae vibrating with concern and admiration.

"Nina," Bella began, "that was brave, what you did out there."

Nina merely shrugged, her voice laced with disappointment. "It was my duty, but it feels like no one else noticed."

Bruno chimed in, "Recognition should be given where it's due, and Nina, you've more than earned it. Your courage should be buzzed out loud, not just for you but for all of us."

Perry agreed, adding, "Visibility in recognition is as important as the act itself. Your bravery should inspire the whole hive. 'Buzz out loud, inspire the crowd,' as it should be."

Bella nodded thoughtfully, her mind abuzz with the new rule. She saw a pattern unfolding, lessons learned that could be applied to create a better hive. Gathering her thoughts, Bella shared the insights she had gathered so far.

"Bruno, Perry, Nina," she began, "Our hive can be so much more if we follow these rules.
- 'Every buzz counts ensuring that everyone gets the recognition they deserve.
- 'Nectar now, Honey later' because recognition should be immediate.
- 'Consistent buzz keeps the hive humming,' reminding us to acknowledge everyone consistently. And
- 'Specific buzz, sweeter honey,' stressing the importance of personalizing recognition."

She looked at each of them, her resolve mirrored in their eyes. "And now, 'Buzz out loud, inspire the crowd.' We need to make recognition visible, for all to see, and get inspired."

As Bella concluded, they sat in shared understanding, the sound of the hive humming around them. This wasn't just about one bee anymore; it was about the future of their hive. It was about making sure that every bee felt seen, heard, and appreciated. And they knew that change was on the horizon. They just had to keep buzzing, louder and together.

Chapter 6: Every bee deserves their buzz

As the summer season advanced, Bella found herself in the new garden she had discovered earlier. The colors were even more vibrant, the fragrance even more intoxicating than she remembered. Bella was joined by Daisy, a young bee who had recently joined the honey-making crew. Daisy, with her bright eyes and enthusiastic hum, was always eager to learn and contribute.

However, Bella noticed that Daisy's once vibrant hum had dulled, her once enthusiastic fluttering now listless. Bella decided to broach the subject while they were both pollinating a particularly vibrant sunflower.

"Daisy," Bella began, her voice soft, "You seem a little quiet today. Is everything alright?"

Daisy sighed, her tiny shoulders drooping. "I just... I don't know, Bella. I work as hard as anyone else in the hive. But it feels like my work isn't noticed because I'm new."

Bella empathized with Daisy's plight. She knew what it felt like to have your contributions overlooked. She gently said, "Daisy, I see your hard work, and it does matter. Every bee, young or old, experienced or new, deserves recognition for their effort. '**Every bee deserves their buzz**.' And I think it's time we reminded our hive of that."

Bella continued, her voice filled with conviction. "You are a part of our hive, Daisy. Your work, your efforts, they all add to our hive's success. It's time we all started acknowledging that."

As the sun began to set, bathing the garden in a warm, golden glow, Bella and Daisy continued their conversation. They discussed the other rules Bella had learned - timely recognition, inclusivity, consistency, specificity, and visibility. Bella emphasized the importance of each rule, their potential to create a more supportive and appreciative hive culture.

By the time they returned to the hive, Daisy looked less forlorn. Her hum had a new undertone of hope, her wings fluttering with renewed vigor. The conversation with Bella had lifted her spirits, making her feel seen and appreciated.

And Bella, seeing the change in Daisy, felt a renewed sense of purpose. She was determined to ensure that every bee, irrespective of their age or role, felt valued and appreciated. Because every bee did deserve their buzz. As the moonlight bathed the hive, Bella knew that the journey to transform their hive was far from over, but each step, each conversation, was a step in the right direction.

Chapter 7: Values in our buzz, unity in our hive.

As the last rays of the summer sun painted the sky with hues of golden amber, Bella found herself in the company of Bruno, Daisy, and Carlos the caretaker. Carlos was a quiet bee, meticulous in his duties, and deeply committed to the well-being of the hive. They were in the heart of the hive, the chamber where honey was stored, a space that reflected Carlos' unyielding dedication and care.

"Bella," Bruno murmured, admiration evident in his voice, "See how Carlos coordinates everything so efficiently? He ensures that every drop of honey is stored properly, that every space is used optimally." Bella watched Carlos with appreciation. His tireless work was a reflection of the hive's core values - unity, diligence, and collective welfare. However, Bella noticed a disparity in how Carlos' recognition was delivered. It was always about his efficiency, never about the values that drove him.

"Bruno, Daisy," Bella began, her voice calm yet assertive, "Do you see how Carlos embodies our hive's values? His work isn't just about being efficient. It's about unity, working for the collective welfare of us all."

Daisy tilted her head thoughtfully. "You're right, Bella. We've been overlooking that in our recognition."

Carlos, upon hearing his name, buzzed over. His antennae twitched curiously as Bella addressed him, "Carlos, we've been admiring your work. But more than just your efficiency, we appreciate how you embody our hive's values."

Carlos blinked in surprise, then his wings fluttered in a hum of quiet gratitude. "Thank you, Bella. The hive's values guide me, but I didn't think anyone noticed."

Bella smiled, a warmth radiating from her. "Well, we do notice, Carlos. And we're going to make sure that from now on, our recognition reflects our hive's values. **'Values in our buzz, unity in our hive.'**"

As they continued their tasks in the warm glow of the hive, a new understanding resonated among them. Recognition wasn't just about acknowledging hard work; it was about honoring the values that fueled such commitment. It was about creating unity in the hive, one buzz at a time.

Chapter 8: Change the buzz, change the hive

The hive buzzed with a new energy as autumn began to tinge the leaves with vibrant colors. Changes had started to ripple through their home, small shifts that were gradually painting a bigger picture. It all began with conversations - conversations inspired by Bella and her newfound principles of recognition.

Bella, Bruno, Daisy, Nina, and Carlos gathered at the center of the hive, amidst the rhythmic hum of diligent workers and the warm glow of stored honey.

"Bella," Bruno began, his voice filled with curiosity, "Ever since we've started following these new principles, I've noticed an increase in our honey production. And it's not just that; everyone seems... happier."

Bella hummed in agreement. "That's right, Bruno. Recognition isn't just about boosting morale; it's about fostering productivity and unity. 'Change the buzz, change the hive.'"

Nina chimed in, her voice strong and clear, "And it's not just us who've noticed, Bella. More bees are joining in, contributing their efforts, their ideas. Our hive is thriving."

Carlos added, his voice softer but no less certain, "We've seen that when our hard work and dedication to the hive's values are recognized, it motivates us to contribute even more."

Daisy fluttered her wings eagerly, "Yes, and it's not just about our work. I feel more connected, more part of the hive than before. We all do."

Bella listened to their observations, her heart buzzing with a warmth that spread to every corner of her tiny bee body. The changes were working. Their hive was transforming, and it all started with the right kind of recognition.

"Bruno, Nina, Carlos, Daisy," Bella said, her voice resonating with the newfound energy of their hive, "Our hive is changing, and it's because of each one of us. We've been able to create a culture of timely, frequent, specific, visible, inclusive, and values-based recognition."

Bella looked around at her friends, her hive, her family, "And as we keep following these principles, our hive will continue to thrive, continue to change. Remember, change the buzz, change the hive."

As the sun set and the hive hummed with the busyness of bees returning home, there was a newfound harmony. The hive was changing, transforming. And at the heart of it all was Bella, the tiny bee with the great vision, steadily guiding her hive towards a brighter, happier future.

Chapter 9: The Queens' Address

The leaves had fallen, and the hive was ablaze with the excitement of a successful harvest season. The time had come for the Queen's annual "State of the Hive" address. Every bee buzzed in anticipation, their wings reflecting the golden light of stored honey. But this year was different. This year, they had something more to celebrate.

The Queen, majestic and graceful, addressed the hive, "My beloved bees, we have accomplished much this season, and our hive is not just busier, but happier, more united."

Her eyes found Bella in the crowd. "Much of this change is due to Bella's vision. Her timely insights and commitment to our hive have enriched us. She reminded us that our buzz, our work, has value and deserves recognition."

A hum of agreement reverberated through the hive, and Bella felt a rush of warmth. The Queen had not just recognized her work, but also acknowledged the principles she advocated for.

The Queen turned her gaze towards Bruno, "And Bruno, your frequent support and consistent hard work have not gone unnoticed. Your dedicated service, especially during the tough days of summer, has been instrumental to our hive's success."

The hive echoed with applause, and Bruno's antennae twitched in surprise, then delight. The Queen had not only recognized him, but she had done so in a specific, visible manner that resonated with every bee present.

Next, the Queen acknowledged Daisy, "Young Daisy, your contribution might seem insignificant to you, but you've played an important role in our hive's growth. Every bee here matters, every effort is appreciated."

Bella watched as her hive celebrated, buzzed with happiness, respect, and appreciation. She was part of this change. Her hive had transformed, and so had she. She now understood what it truly meant to 'buzz well, live well.'

The Queen concluded, "Our hive has not just changed, it has transformed. And it is due to every one of us here. Remember, my beloved bees, to 'buzz well, live well.'"

As the hive echoed with the Queen's words, Bella felt a profound sense of fulfillment. She was home, in a hive that wasn't just buzzing with activity but with respect and appreciation, a hive that truly understood the power of recognition. And for Bella, there was no better feeling.

Chapter 10: The path of the hive.

Spring returned to the meadow, blanketing the world in hues of blossoming colors. Bella's hive was more vibrant than ever, pulsating with the renewed energy of a hive transformed. The changes Bella had inspired were no longer just practices but had become the way of life.

Throughout the year, Bella watched with pride as the principles she advocated became the guiding lights for every bee in the hive. They brought about positive changes that even Bella hadn't anticipated.
The hive's honey production was at an all-time high, thanks to the diligent efforts of the worker bees and their enthusiasm to contribute. Bees were happier and healthier, the camaraderie was stronger, and each day buzzed with positivity. Every bee, from the oldest to the youngest, felt included and valued, reinforcing the unity and harmony in their hive.

Recognition was frequent and timely, and it was specific to each bee's unique contribution. It echoed throughout the hive, fostering a culture of respect and appreciation. Most importantly, it reflected the values of the hive, strengthening the bond among them and their collective commitment to their home.

The Queen, too, was a part of this journey. She not only acknowledged but practiced the principles, ensuring they were deeply rooted in the hive's culture.

As Bella watched her hive thrive, she knew their journey wasn't over. It was a constant endeavor, an ongoing commitment to uphold the principles she introduced, to "keep the buzz going, keep the hive glowing."

The Hives Rules:

As the sun set on another year, Bella couldn't help but reflect on the journey so far. The transformation, the growth, the unity - all a testament to the power of recognition. She quietly murmured the rules to herself, each one resonating with the heart of their hive:

- Hive Rule 1: **"Every Buzz Counts"** - Every member of our hive is crucial, and their work must be recognized immediately when they make an impact, no matter how big or small.

- Hive Rule 2: **"Nectar Now, Not Later"** - Don't delay in acknowledging a job well done. Timely appreciation is vital to keep our hive healthy and humming.

- Hive Rule 3: **"A consistent buzz keeps the hive humming.."** - Regular recognition of each other's efforts is essential for maintaining morale and a positive environment in our hive.

- Hive Rule 4: **"Specific buzz, sweeter honey"** - Tailor your acknowledgment to what was accomplished. Specific recognition is more meaningful and satisfying.

- Hive Rule 5: **"Buzz out loud, inspire the crowd"** - Don't be shy about giving recognition. Public acknowledgment inspires others and strengthens our hive.

- Hive Rule 6: **"Every bee deserves their buzz"** - Include everyone in our recognition program. Every single bee in our hive is crucial to our success.

- Hive Rule 7: **"Values in our buzz, unity in our hive"** - Our hive's recognition should reflect our shared values. This brings us closer as a community and strengthens our unity.

- Hive Rule 8: **"Change the buzz, change the hive"** - If we want to improve our hive, we must first improve how we acknowledge each other's contributions.

- Hive Rule 9: **"Keep the buzz going, keep the hive glowing"** - Continual recognition not only sustains our current success but also fosters growth for our hive's future.

With these rules echoing in her heart, Bella knew that as long as they followed these principles, their hive would continue to flourish.

Her journey continued, but she wasn't alone. She had her hive, her family, with her, ready to uphold their new culture and ensure their hive thrived under these principles.

Bella

for more information and worksheets go to:
ChangeTheHive.com

www.ingramcontent.com/pod-product-compliance
Lightning Source LLC
Chambersburg PA
CBHW031559210526
45464CB00003B/1352